Picasso

Picasso

Robin Langley Sommer

JG
PRESS

Previous page: Portrait of Marie-Thérèse (6 January 1937)
Oil on canvas
25⅜×31⅞in (100×81cm)
Picasso Museum

Reprinted 2004 by
World Publications Group, Inc.
455 Somerset Avenue
North Dighton, MA 02764
www.wrldpub.com

ISBN 1-57215-373-3

Printed and bound in China by
Leefung-Asco Printers Trading Ltd

10 9 8 7 6 5

CONTENTS

PORTRAIT
OF THE
ARTIST

Born in 1881, Pablo Picasso's long career has an enduring fascination for our restless, fragmented age. The clarity of his vision, the courage of his radical departures from artistic convention, the sheer productivity of his working life, his mastery of an incredible variety of media — painting, sculpture, engraving, ceramics, drawing — have awed admirers and detractors alike. What was the source of this enormous creativity? In 1971 his friend Jean Leymarie suggested in the tribute *Picasso: The Artist of the Century,* written two years before the artist's death, that 'he prevails over time by living and working constantly in the *present.*'

It was Gertrude Stein who said that 'Cubism is a purely Spanish conception and only Spaniards can be Cubists.' While this statement is not entirely fair to the French Cubists, including Georges Braque, Picasso's intimate friend and associate during the early years in Paris, there is a valid insight here: it is impossible to dissociate Pablo Ruiz Picasso from his native land. Picasso was born on 25 October 1881 in the Mediterranean seaport of Malaga, where his father José Ruiz Blasco was an artist and a teacher of painting and drawing at the School of Arts and Crafts in the province of Andalusia. The artist's boyhood was spent in the landscape that would appear again and again in his works.

In 1891 Picasso's family moved to the Atlantic seaport of Corunna, where his father obtained a teaching appointment at La Guarda Institute. The climate of Corunna was colder and damper than that of Malaga, but it proved congenial to the young Picasso, who had already shown an extraordinary aptitude for drawing. His biographer Robert Maillard, who collaborated with art historian Frank Elgar on the 1956 study *Picasso,* states that from around the age of seven 'he was never without a pencil in his hand, and was already arousing his parents' admiration.' Six years later the boy was so enthusiastic that in 1894 Don José gave up painting altogether and solemnly presented all his colors and brushes to his son. When the family resettled in Barcelona the following year, the young Picasso was on the verge of being admitted to the Barcelona Province Art School, *La Lonja,*

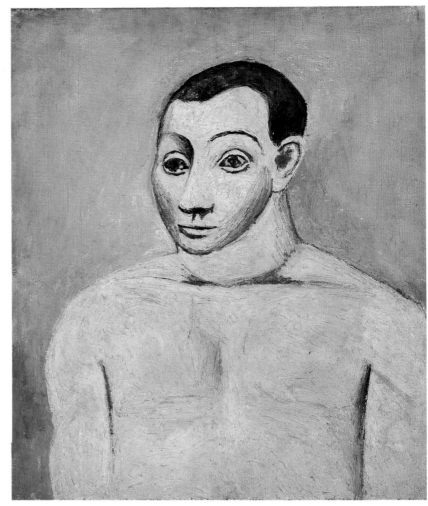

Left: This self-portrait, painted in 1906, displays some of the influences so important to Picasso's work: the face is treated almost like a mask and the exaggerated proportions of the eyes, nose and eyebrows show the influence of Iberian art. Picasso Museum, Paris.

Right: Portrait of the Artist's Mother (1896). This pastel portrait reveals Picasso's technical ability in handling the materials and his ability to capture a likeness at the age of just fourteen. Picasso Museum, Barcelona.

Below left: Portrait of Lola (1899). One of Picasso's favorite models at this period was his sister Lola. This portrait shows Picasso's indebtedness to the Impressionists. Both subject and treatment are comparable to works by Monet, Renoir and Degas. Here Picasso's signature reads P Ruiz Picasso. Picasso Museum, Barcelona.

Below far left: The Riera de Sant Joan, Seen from a Window (1900). One of Picasso's studios in Barcelona was in the Riera de Sant Joan, which he shared with his friend Carlos Casagemas. Picasso spent most of his early years living in towns and consequently his landscapes are often views from the windows of his studios, placed high up in the building and overlooking rooftops, or the long perspective of the streets below. Picasso Museum, Barcelona.

where his father was teaching. In 1896 he completed in a day the task set for the entrance examination, for which a month was allowed. Although his father's spirits had sunk with the move to Barcelona, he was determined to encourage his son in every way, and soon afterward rented a studio for him in the Calle de la Plata. It was there that the young artist painted the canvas *Science and Charity,* in which a patient on a sickbed is attended by a doctor and a nun. Don José himself sat for the portrait of the doctor, and it is a testimony to their mutual attachment that all his life Picasso painted most of his paternal figures as bearded like his father. Impressive likenesses of his mother Maria Lopez Picasso and of his sister Lola were also made during the mid-1890s. By the age of 20 he had achieved artistic maturity.

In 1897, at the advice of Picasso's Uncle Salvador, he was sent to Madrid to continue his studies. The Royal Academy of San Fernando accepted him readily, but he was soon dissatisfied with the constraints of official instruction and returned to Barcelona. A winter illness in 1898 threatened his health, and his friend Manuel Pallarés took him home to his native village of Horta de Ebro (now Horta de San Juan) in Aragon. There Picasso discovered a deep love of the simple, outdoor life of the local people and an appreciation for the simple integrity of the country craftsmen. 'Everything I know,' he declared later in life, 'I learned in the village of Pallarés.'

Back in the thriving cultural community of Barcelona, Picasso soon became part of the young modernist group which congregated at the cabaret *Els Quatre Gats* (the Four Cats) modeled on the Parisian Chat Noir, rediscovered El Greco, and welcomed all the various currents of European thought, from Nietzsche to the French Impressionists. In this café society Picasso formed lasting friendships with other young intellectuals, including Angel and Mateo Fernandez de Soto, poet Jamime Sabartés, painters Carlos Casagemas and Sebastian Junyer, and sculptor Julio Gonzalez. He drew their portraits and his own as the impulse took him and plunged deeply into Barcelona's artistic renaissance.

At this time the stylistic current of the German-style Art Nouveau *Jugendstil* found appeal in the Spanish temperament. From Munich *Jugend* and *Simplicissimus,* the foremost journals of *Jugendstil,* were read by Spanish artists. According to Leymarie, in 1901 Picasso 'tried to extend the movement to Madrid and founded there a "sincere" art magazine, *Arte Joven,* in which, alongside impassioned declarations, appeared Goethe's luminous profession of faith in universal harmony . . . together with a significant study of the "psychology of the guitar, symbol of the popular soul and symbol of emotions, which may be why it has the shape of a woman." ' Both woman and guitar would be constant elements in his work.

Finding Madrid too conservative for his taste, Picasso made the obligatory pilgrimage to Paris for the first time in 1900, with his friend Casagemas, and sold three bull-ring scenes (already one of his major themes) to the dealer Berthe Weill. He received 100 francs for them. During his stay, Picasso became acquainted with the works of the masters of modern French painting, especially Renoir. He studied the color schemes of the Neoimpressionists, and he was influenced by Degas and Toulouse-Lautrec's subjects of the 'social milieu' — barmaids, outcasts, and beggars.

Above: Famille de Saltimbanques (1905). In 1905, new themes of strolling performers and harlequins were introduced into Picasso's works. He had been a regular visitor to the Cirque Medrano in Montmartre and developed friendships with many of the characters he drew. Like Degas, Picasso portrays his entertainers both during their performances and, as here, their private, backstage lives. Picasso Museum, Paris.

Left: The etching *The Frugal Repast* (1904) belongs to Picasso's Blue Period. The theme of blindness appears in this and many other works (cf. *Blind Man's Meal,* 1903). The treatment of the hands is interesting; their elongation and exaggeration would seem to compensate for the loss of sight. Private collection.

At Christmas he returned to Spain, and in May 1901 his friends in Barcelona organized an exhibition of his work at the *Sala Pares.* Miguel Utrillo reviewed it favorably in the journal *Pel y Ploma (Fur and Feather),* noting perceptively that 'The art of Picasso is very young, the child of his spirit of observation, which does not pardon the weaknesses of the people of our time, and brings out even the beauties of the horrible, which he notes with the sobriety of one who draws because he sees and not because he can do a nose from memory.'

It was after his second trip to Paris in 1901 that the young artist dropped his father's surname and began to sign all his work with his mother's name only. His friend Sabartés pointed out that this was due not to any coldness toward his father, but because 'his father's name, Ruiz, was very common, whereas the name Picasso was so unusual that it seemed ideally suited for a man whom they [his friends] wanted to single out, and whose nature set him apart from all others.'

The melancholy pictures of his Blue Period, beginning in 1901, reflect the poverty and isolation he experienced in both Paris and Barcelona over the next several years. ('I have no idea whether I'm a great painter,' he once said to the poet Max Jacob, 'but I am a great draftsman.') The paintings of the Blue Period are essentially figurative works. The people are from Lautrec's world, but in Picasso's treatment there is an emphasis on expressive gestures like those of Renoir's figures. He tended toward social criticism, which since Zola published *l'Assommoir* in 1877 had been taken up by many artists, including Forain and the German, Kathe Kolwitz. Color in this period is reduced to a single dominant tone, blue. Once again, in this treatment of homogenous color Picasso was not alone. Both Odilon Redon and Eugène Carrière treat color in a way expressive of feelings or emotions.

In 1904, when Picasso settled in Paris at the Bateau-Lavoir, a warren of dilapidated studios whose tenants frequented the Lapin Agile cabaret, he continued to paint the attenuated portraits of blind men, laundresses and outcasts whose prevailing mood and color were blue. With his meeting of Max Jacob in 1904 through the art dealer Vollard, Picasso was introduced to life in Bohemian Montmartre. Here he met the Spanish painter Juan Gris, was introduced to African art by André Derain, and even received the occasional visit from Degas.

Undoubtedly, Picasso's sympathies were attuned to those whose poverty and loneliness he was sharing. The colorful street scenes, bull-fights and portraits of the previous years were superseded by these monochromatic works for which there was little demand. It was during this period that Sabartés observed Picasso at work and recorded his impression of that concentration which would characterize the artist throughout his life: 'His attention is torn between canvas and palette, but it never leaves either: both stand in his line of sight and he discerns them together. He gives himself body and soul to the work which is the justification of his existence . . . all his senses focused on the sole object before him, as if in the grip of a spell.' Many years later, Picasso himself would observe that 'Nothing can be done without solitude. I made for myself a solitude unsuspected by anyone.'

At this time the 22-year-old artist made his first major etching, *The Frugal Repast,* which echoed the melancholy note struck by his predominantly blue canvases. It was also in 1904 that Picasso formed his relationship with Fernande Olivier, who would be his model and mistress for the next seven years.

By 1905 Picasso was working on themes of strolling player, harlequins and circus performers where the color was still homogenous, but shifted to pinks and terracottas. Contrasts were avoided, and only in certain areas would the colors be varied – in harlequins' costumes or baskets of flowers. The figures, outlined against the background, are reminiscent of Puvis de Chevanne and of Gauguin's cloisonnism. The music-hall themes of Lautrec mixed with the ballet world of Degas come together in Picasso's *Les Saltimbanques.*

Around 1905, among the Fauves in particular, but apparent in European art in general, was a so-called 'new spirit of freedom' in which artists sought newer and more powerful means of expression via a return to more primitive sources of art. Picasso found such sources in his native Spanish traditions: the ritual of the bullfight, the expressive paintings of El Greco, and ancient Iberian Art, especially pieces from the Osuna excavations which were shown at the Louvre in 1906. A visit to the Musée Ethnographie du Trocadero, possibly made in 1907, and Picasso's acquisition of primitive art forms provided background for his work in these years, in which his figures became archaic and sculptural.

This tendency in art was not uncommon; at the same time, around 1905 Derain, Vlaminck and Matisse (who Picasso would meet at Gertrude Stein's 'salon') were also searching out primitive and, especially, African art. In Dresden, Kirchener was studying the collections in the Zwingers' department of ethnography. In Munich, Kandinsky was studying the primitive works of Bavarian peasants. The emphasis that has been laid on Picasso's interest in primitive art forms can be misleading. The interest he showed was symptomatic of a general trend in European art. But in his use of primitive

elements, Picasso would develop a new pictorial structure. The primitive influence is seen in Picasso's sculptures, for several of which Fernande served as the model, and in the early Cubist works of 1907. Picasso was one of the first twentieth-century painters to cross the sharp line that had separated painting from sculpture during the nineteenth century.

Other notable events of 1905 included Picasso's meeting with the poet Guillaume Apollinaire, who published a glowing article about the young artist in *La Plume* that May. In spring 1906 his circle of acquaintances had come to include Gertrude Stein. The American expatriate was one of his first influential patrons, and he painted his well-known portrait of her in 1906, after he had turned away from the somber subjects of the Blue Period to paint the harlequins, acrobats, and actors of his Rose, or Circus, Period. Stein and her brother Leo had settled in France in 1904, and the writer knew nothing about the artist when she bought his canvas *Girl with a Basket of Flowers* in the rue Laffitte. She was eager to meet him and called at the ramshackle Bateau-Lavoir, where she promptly bought 800 francs worth of pictures. This welcome event secured the friendship of the 'Picassos,' as Stein called Pablo and Fernande, and they became frequent visitors to the rue de Fleurus. Other early patrons included Wilhelm Uhde and Ambroise Vollard, who would be the subject of an important Cubist portrait in 1909.

The year 1907 was crucial in the development of the 26-year-old artist,

Above: Self Portrait (1907) is remarkable for its disregard of traditional European art forms. Picasso depicts a full face, or frontal, eye in the manner of Egyptian art. The distortions to the nose and ears are influenced by Iberian sculpture. The whole effect is one of stillness similar to that found in Archaic Greek 'Kouros' figures. Gallery of the Twentieth Century, Berlin.

Right: In spring 1906 Picasso met the American author Gertrude Stein, who was to become one of his first influential patrons. The photograph also shows Picasso's portrait of her.

Left: The concentration on volume, the compositional structure and the treatment of the shallow picture space of *Les Grandes Baigneuses* by Paul Cézanne (1839-1906) were to influence Picasso's *Demoiselles d'Avignon.* Petit Palais.

Above: Where do we come from? What are we? Where are we going? (1897) by Paul Gauguin. Gauguin was, for many artists of his generation and after, the archetypal figure of the artist as 'free spirit.' It is in his use of color that his main influence appears in Picasso's work, of 'cloisonnism' — outlines of dark pigment containing lightly modeled color. Tompkins collection, Boston Museum of Fine Arts.

Right: Georges Braque, seen here in Paris in 1922, was introduced to Picasso by Guillaume Apollinaire in 1907. It was through Braque's work, particularly a series of landscapes exhibited at the Salon des Indépendants in 1909, that the name 'Cubism' was coined. Braque later introduced Picasso to texturing and *papier collé.*

Left: Château de Médan (c 1880) by Cézanne. Note the technique used: the foliage is painted using systematic diagonal brushstrokes which vary in color but are repeated in direction. This use of directional strokes gives a unity and order to the subject, and can also be found in Picasso's works in the early 'Cubist' stages, in particular landscapes and still-lifes. Burrell collection.

now increasingly attracted to the work of Paul Cézanne, whose work had been introduced to him by Vollard. The triumphant retrospective of Cézanne's paintings and drawings at the Salon d'Automne, combined with Picasso's heightened awareness of African and Oceanian art, were direct causal influences on the creation of *Les Demoiselles d'Avignon*. For many years the canvas remained rolled up in Picasso's studio. It was reproduced for the first time in *La Revolution Surréaliste* in 1925 but was not publicly exhibited until 1937. The title of the painting, according to tradition, was given some years later by André Salmon, who evidently remarked on the similarity of the figures in the work to women from a brothel in the carrer D'Avinyo in Barcelona. The composition was altered many times; early studies included a female figure with a thick plait of hair, believed to be

based on Marie Laurencin, who was a contemporary around the Bateau-Lavoir. The central figure was originally that of a sailor, surrounded by women, fruit and flowers, while from the side a second sailor entered carrying a skull. In the final composition the sailors have vanished and there remain only the women and a still-life of fruit.

Work started on *Demoiselles D'Avignon* in 1907, after Picasso had assimilated the formal lessons of Cézanne and began concentrating on the study of volume, space and light. (In 1908, during Picasso's visit to Horta de Ebro, the fragmenting of solid surfaces into facets would be perfected.) The compositional structure of *Demoiselles* was also influenced by Cézanne, in particular his *Grandes Baigneuses,* as well as this treatment of the shallow picture space. The decorative color treatment however belongs to Gauguin. In overall appearance *Demoiselles* is close to a classical figurative composition – three of the five female figures are recognizable even if distorted – but the details betray a complete departure from the conventions of Western art. The figure on the left has its origins in Iberian art. The barbaric Greek period of the peninsula is revealed in the enlargement of the chin and ears, and the outlined frontal eye. On the right, the figures' heads are distorted into mask-like features, familiar to Picasso from the sculptures of French Colonial Africa.

The form and composition, though, shows the influence of Cézanne. Cézanne's fundamental principle was that the artist should develop pictorial compositions based on the direct observation of nature, and then apply his conception *to* nature. From this principle Cézanne arrived at his often quoted belief (which was published in 1906 by Emile Bernard) that nature should be treated in terms of geometric forms like spheres, cones and cylinders. What Cézanne was advocating was a method of translating the order that could be found in nature into forms that could give nature a permanence that could be embodied in painting. By the analysis of nature the form could be found, and from this 'analytical' approach new forms of expression could be discovered. In studying Cézanne's ideals, the formal method of analytical Cubism would emerge.

It was *Demoiselles,* which scandalized his friends and associates, that brought about Picasso's friendship with the German-born art dealer Daniel-Henry Kahnweiler, who would become his friend and handle his work for the duration of his career. Wilhelm Uhde took Kahnweiler to see the unfinished painting shortly after the dealer opened his gallery at rue Vignon, and he was profoundly impressed by it. At about the same time, Apollinaire introduced Picasso to Georges Braque, with whom he would share so much during the next few years. Braque had been connected with the Fauvist painters, but had started to rework their aesthetics after studying Cézanne's work and African sculpture. Basically, Braque had arrived independently at similar conclusions to Picasso.

In 1908 Braque visited L'Estaque, near Marseilles, where he began applying Cézannesque principles of analysis. The landscapes he produced were submitted to the Salon d'Automne, but were rejected by the jury. Matisse, who had been a member of the jury, spoke of a landscape of cubes, and the art critic Louis Vauxcelles referred to the L'Estaque landscapes at the Salon des Indépendants in 1909 as 'Cubical oddities.' Cubism was christened.

Picasso's interest in form led him naturally to sculpture. In his three-

dimensional explorations he would use a variety of techniques ranging from wood carvings and modeling in clay and plaster of paris to the less conventional assemblages, imprintings and cuttings. The first wooden sculptures date from around 1906-07. This technique was then neglected by most artists, excepting, of course, Gauguin, whose works Picasso had become familiar with by 1901. A revived interest occurred in Gauguin's work particularly after the Salon d'Automne retrospective exhibition in 1906. Following this, Picasso's carvings became more primitive in character, carving technique and in design.

From 1909 to 1915 an intensified interest in form leads to the bronze *Head of a Woman (Fernande),* constructed in what seem to be shattered planes. In Picasso's painting, volumes had to be flattened out and 'broken' in order to be accommodated two-dimensionally, but in three dimensions, the sculpture allowed methods of using planes to accomplish volume. In the period 1910 to 1925 Picasso would produce *The Glass of Absinthe* (1914), a painted bronze and the only piece from this period done in the round.

By 1911 the fortunes of the 'Picassos' were greatly improved. Gertrude Stein recounts their move from the old studio in the rue Ravignan to an apartment in the boulevard Clichy: 'Fernande began to buy furniture and have a servant . . . Fernande had at this time a new friend of whom she often spoke to me. This was Eva, who was living with Marcoussis. One evening all four of them come to the rue de Fleurus.' Fernande soon had reason to regret her enthusiasm for the small, vivid Eva Gouel; she quickly forsook Marcoussis for Picasso, who fell deeply in love with her. In 1912 they traveled to Avignon and Sorgues together, moving on when their idyll was interrupted by unwelcome friends. Leymarie says that Picasso wrote Kahnweiler, with whom he had recently signed his first three-year contract, to say that 'I love her very much and I shall write her name on my pictures.' The *Ma Jolie* series, painted before the Great War, was a tribute to Eva.

By this time, it could safely be said that the impact of the new aesthetics was so great that no Western artist could be unaffected by it. Already by 1909 Albert Gliezes, Jean Metzinger, Francis Picabia, Auguste Herbin, Henri le Fauconnier and André Lhote, who had 'discovered' Cézanne via the Impressionists, commenced work according to Cubist principles. In 1910 Robert Delaunay, Louis Marcoussis, Roger de le Fresnaye, Marcel Duchamp, Fernand Léger and Juan Gris, who had continued to paint in a style derivative of Lautrec (despite having shared Picasso's studio since 1906), joined the movement. By 1912 Cubist innovations would be reflected by a wide range of artists in their individual manner. And after the visit to Paris of the Russian artist Vladimir Tatlin in 1913, the gospel of Cubism gained converts in the East as well. Impressed by the musical instruments of tin and cardboard that he saw in Picasso's studio, Tatlin returned to Moscow to experiment with reliefs constructed from building materials.

Picasso seemed to take his new renown in his stride. To critical eval-

Above: Head of a Woman (1909) shows Picasso's interest in sculpture.
Below right: Seated Woman (1909). The body is built up of well-defined facets and a sense of solidity is achieved through the use of almost monochromatic modeling.
Below: Head of a Woman (Fernande), 1909. Picasso Museum, Paris.
Far right: Sleeping Women with Shutters (25 April 1936). Picasso Museum, Paris.

uations of Cubism, he responded wryly that 'If cubism is an art of transition, I am sure that the only thing that will come out of it is another form of cubism.' And Gertrude Stein, referring to herself in the third person in *The Autobiography of Alice B Toklas,* wrote that 'she always says about young painters, about anything, once everybody knows they are good the adventure is over. And adds Picasso with a sigh, even after everybody knows they are good, not any more people really like them than they did when only the few knew they were good.'

In the spring of 1914, Picasso left the rue Schoelcher, where he and Eva had shared a studio apartment, for Montrouge. Stein says that 'His friends, a great many of them . . . followed him to Montparnasse but it was not the same. The intimacy with Braque was waning and of his old friends the only ones he saw frequently were Guillaume Apollinaire and Gertrude Stein.' Picasso's happiness at this time was clouded not only by the war, but by the declining health of Eva, who died the following year.

In 1916 Picasso met the brilliant young poet Jean Cocteau, who introduced him to the world of the Russian Ballet. Leymarie says that Picasso, 'who had always been fascinated by the stage, collaborated all the more eagerly when he married one of Sergei Diaghilev's dancers [Olga Koklova, in 1917]. That year he designed the striking scenery and costumes for *Parade,* which was the occasion for his first trip to Italy.' Cocteau's idea of a modern ballet, first performed in Paris on 17 May 1917 at the Théâtre du Chatelet, would have music by Erik Satie, designs by Picasso and choreography by Massine. Picasso's designs, only partly influenced by Cubism, returned to earlier themes of harlequins and the circus.

Cocteau's idea was to have a front curtain that would be entertaining but would keep the audience unaware and unprepared for the ballet itself, which would prove itself to be a strong attack on conventionality, bringing a violent reaction from ballet audiences brought up on classical repertoire. In the preface to the programs Apollinaire called the mixture of realism and fantasy – 'surrealism.' Two years later, Manuel de Falla's production of *The Three-Cornered Hat,* with its Spanish theme, inspired a drop-curtain design of the bull ring; bull fighting was one of the several passions Picasso had shared with his father.

In the early 1920s Picasso developed two apparently conflicting styles. The first was a realistic tendency with classical themes, depicting large figures of a sculptural quality. This style actually forms part of a general tendency in European art at this time to 'reconstruct' the outward appearances of reality. After World War I, the ideological climate of Europe understandably favored a return to the traditional values of order and balance – in life as well as in art. An entire generation of writers and artists would be profoundly influenced by re-interpreting antiquity. Picasso was not alone in his classicism; Cocteau's *Antigone* and Stravinsky's *Oedipus Rex* bear witness to this political and artistic climate. What is peculiar, nevertheless, is Picasso's own style. In a way similar to the sixteenth century mannerists, like Parmigianino's *Madonna with the Long Neck,* he elongates figures, and broadens and acutely foreshortens limbs.

Alongside this neo-classical style, Picasso was producing a series of Cubist paintings of still-lifes and harlequins, culminating in 1921 in two versions of *Three Musicians.* Both versions represent three masked figures. A pierrot plays the clarinet, a harlequin the guitar, and a monk sings. The composition resembles a stage, and the large forms are nearly all geometrical, pieced together in a 'synthetic' technique. The two paintings differ in that the dog appears only in New York's Metropolitan Museum version.

Leymarie also remarks that the birth of Picasso's first son, Paulo, in February 1921 marked a new cycle of *Maternités* different from the earlier Blue and Rose periods. *Family by the Sea* has been said to reflect Picasso's introduction to family life, and this was followed by portraits of his son dressed as a harlequin and a pierrot.

Thus the early 1920s were marked by profound changes in outlook, relating to Picasso's new family, and in general a feeling of restlessness and growing anxiety. During the 1920s religion and philosophy would develop ideas that eventually gave rise to Surrealism and Existentialism. Around 1925 Picasso's style reflects a change that would bring his works closer to Surrealism by including absurd and even monstrous motifs and themes.

In 1931, to escape from the troubles of married life, Picasso set up a studio

in a country house in Boisgeloup that gave him the space he needed to try a new approach to sculpture. He asked his long-time friend Julio Gonzalez to teach him the techniques of metal sculpture, and during the early 1930s he produced some 50 different pieces, including the assemblages of various ready-made objects and materials – the extension of Collage Cubism into three-dimensional constructions. The British artist, critic and collector Roland Penrose, a friend of the artist, relates that 'Pieces of scrap-iron, springs, saucepan lids, sieves, bolts and screws picked out with discernment from the rubbish heap could mysteriously take their place in these constructions and convincingly come to life with a new personality. The vestiges of their origins remained visible as witnesses to the transformation that the magician had brought about, a challenge to the identity of anything and everything.' According to Herbert Read, from 1930 onward, Picasso 'is concerned to represent in his figures certain vital forces of social significance – the *anima* that we project into all subjects, animate or inanimate.' With Picasso at Boisgeloup was Marie-Thérèse Walter, whom he had met by accident in 1927 and whom was now his mistress, foremost model, and who would bear him a daughter, Maya, in 1935. Marie's image was to dominate the period 1931 to 1936 in both Picasso's paintings and sculptures, in a series of seated and sleeping nudes including *The Dream* (1932) and *Girl Before a Mirror* (1932).

In these paintings rounded forms and curves are used, which demonstrate Marie-Thérèse's monumental sculptural quality. Paintings of her are linked to the sculpture; they are pictorial parallels to the three-dimensional works. During the early 1930s Picasso also produced graphic work, illustrating Balzac's *Chef D'oeuvre Inconnu* and Ovid's *Metamorphoses* as well as poems by his friends Tristan Tzara and Paul Eluard. Picasso had also started writing poetry himself in Spanish and French, and would be published in May 1936 by the Surrealist André Breton in a special edition of *Cahiers d'Art*.

The mid-1930s were turbulent years for Picasso, not only because of his domestic crises, but because of inner conflict about his long absence from Spain, which he visited for the last time in 1934. In the work of this period, actual scenes of Spanish bullfighting are dramatically combined with the antique, legendary cycle of the Minotaur.

The complications of his personal life, torn between Olga and Paulo and Marie-Thérèse and Maya, are also reflected in several drawings of the mid-1930s, which Picasso himself described as 'the worst time in my life.' Leymarie points out that in several major wash drawings of this period, 'the family group centering on the child is represented in mythological guise.' In 1936, these problems were exacerbated by Paul Eluard's introduction to Picasso of Dora Maar (born Markovich), the Yugoslavian photographer who shared his passion for his work – always his first love.

Above: Pablo Picasso (1935), photographed by Man Ray. As Picasso's own work became increasingly 'Surreal' it is appropriate that this portrait was taken by the leading Surrealist photographer.

Above: Armed supporters of the Republican cause in 1936, during the Spanish Civil War. The theme of weeping women would occur in Picasso's work constantly through the war years and after.

Right: Taken in 1936 during the Spanish Civil War, this photograph shows government troops on the Cathedral of Siguenza firing on rebels in an attempt to stop their advance on Madrid.

Left: Picasso (second right) at Antibes in 1937 with Dora Maar (extreme right), the Yugoslavian photographer who Picasso met in 1936. In front is the photographer Man Ray.

At the outbreak of the Spanish Civil War, Picasso was vehement in his opposition to the takeover of the government by General Francisco Franco. Picasso's support for the Republicans was recognized by his being named director of the Prado Museum. In April 1937, the Basque town of Guernica was raided by bombers of the German Condor Legion under the orders of Franco. Picasso at this time was working on a commission from the Spanish Democratic Government, a wall mural for the Spanish Pavilion at the Paris World's Fair. This commission and worldwide condemnation of Franco's act would give rise to *Guernica,* which Janson has so accurately described as an evocation of 'the agony of total war.'

The 25½-foot mural *Guernica* was completed over a period of several months, and photographed by Dora Maar at every stage of development. In mid-June it was installed in the Spanish Pavilion.

Since the mid-1930s, Picasso's works had become progressively more expressive. Early curving forms had gradually given way to the more dramatically effective angular. Often his subject matter had dealt with themes of destruction, often using symbols of horses and bulls. These animals provided the allegorical framework for *Guernica.* A struggling disemboweled horse at the center of an equilateral triangle built into the composition, becomes the symbol of pain. On the far left, the bull remains fixed and motionless. Between them are the symbols of human suffering; figures fleeing in panic, a woman falling, the body of a fallen fighter. At the top, the figure of a woman enters the picture, holding a lamp. The structure of the pictorial space has the capacity to suggest both an interior and an exterior view, painted in black, white and gray. This realization of an emblematic art – Picasso transposed the event he depicted into emblems and symbols – raises *Guernica* to the state of a universal mythology. By means of pictorial signs, the bombing of Guernica has been made a legend.

In the final years of the decade, Picasso would rework the images of *Guernica* in such paintings as *Weeping Woman.* It is easy to read into these works presentiments of World War II, especially when the artist himself observed darkly at this time that 'with me, a picture is a sum-total of destructions. I make a picture, then I destroy it.'

In all of Picasso's work at this time there is a sense of intense foreboding, as in *Cat Catching a Bird* (1939). The paintings through the war are marked with anguish and despair, but there are also portraits of Dora Maar, who had shared his life since 1936, and his daughter Maya. As the war continued, and the situation in Europe became more catastrophic, Picasso's reactions became intensified. Studies of human heads undergo violent distortions. During the anxious days after the fall of France in 1940, Picasso remained at his Parisian studio in the rue des Grands-Augustins. When a contingent of German officers called upon him and asked to see his work, he gave them a photo of *Guernica.* One of them asked, 'Did you do this?' Picasso replied, 'No, you did.'

Though materials were scarce, Picasso's wartime output was extensive, in both painting and sculpture. In the winter of 1941 Picasso also wrote a short drama, *Desire caught by the Tail,* revealing a deep understanding of the insecurity and weakness of the individual. The work of the war years shows a tenacious adherence to the ordered reality of daily life, which persists in the face of every adversity. It was in 1943 that Picasso produced his arresting assemblage *Bull's Head,* in which the seat of a bicycle served for the animal's head and the handlebars for its horns. Picasso arranged for the assembly to be cast in bronze, believing that the metal would give a sense of unity to the unrelated objects and would disguise their true nature. What we see though, are the actual objects, which at any time could return to their 'proper' use. As Picasso said, *Bull's Head* 'should have been thrown away immediately afterward. Thrown into the street, into the gutter, anywhere . . . Then a working man would come along and pick it up. And he would find that out of this bull's head he might be able to make a bicycle seat and handlebars. And he does so . . . Now *that* would have been wonderful. That is the gift of metamorphosis.'

The year 1943 was also the one in which Picasso met Françoise Gilot, the

young painter with whom he would live after the war ended and who would bear him two children in the late 1940s. The major three-dimensional piece of this period, *Man With Sheep,* is a fully modeled monumental piece. The clay model was made in the studio at the rue des Grands-Augustins and cast in plaster almost immediately, since the model was in danger of collapsing. The stiff, jutting angle of the sheep's head contrasts strongly with the solid, four-square stance of the shepherd, an archetype of endurance. The size and treatment give a classical character to the piece, reinforced by the theme of the 'Good Shepherd,' although Picasso himself denied any symbolic intention. This statue would remain with Picasso to the end of his life, through every change of location and residence.

After the liberation of Paris in August 1944, Picasso announced that he had joined the Communist Party, which elicited a storm of protest at the Salon d'Automne – the first Salon in which the artist had ever shown – in October. Picasso explained his position in an interview published by *New Masses* (New York) a few weeks later. 'I have always been an exile,' he said, 'now I no longer am. Until the day when Spain can welcome me back, the French Communist Party has opened its arms to me, and I have found in it those that I most value, the greatest scientists, the greatest poets, all those beautiful faces of Parisian insurgents that I saw during the August days [of the liberation of Paris]. I am once more among my brothers.' But, like many intellectuals of the time, Picasso soon found himself facing the problems posed by a committed art, and by his refusal to submit to the constraints of Socialist Realism.

After the liberation and the return of old friends from abroad Picasso made his way again to the Mediterranean. Unhappily, his friend Max Jacob was not among those who lived to see the liberation. He had been interned at the concentration camp at Drancy, and died of pneumonia on 5 March 1944. In the months before his departure, Picasso had been working on lithographs of still-lifes and scenes of bull fights. In an extended stay in 1946 at the Château D'Antibes (now the Grimaldi Museum) his subject matter changed dramatically. Legendary figures of nymphs, fauns and satyrs in Arcadian settings appeared.

Picasso also took the Villa La Galloise, an empty house adjacent to the village of Vallauris which had been a pottery-making center since Roman times. In 1947, the year Françoise Gilot gave birth to their son Claude, Picasso became interested in the potteries at Vallauris. The next year witnessed a great production of ceramics similar in treatment to his polychrome sculpture. At the same time, he continued to paint portraits of Françoise (often interpreting her face as a flower or sun), of his son Claude, and daughter Paloma, born in 1949, in brilliant colors and arabesques.

DEUXIÈME
CONGRÈS
MONDIAL
DES PARTISANS
DE LA PAIX
LONDRES
13·19 NOVEMBRE 1950

MOURLOT IMP. PARIS

Picasso's presence in Vallauris brought a new prosperity to the town, which was much appreciated by its inhabitants. The life-size bronze *Man with Sheep* was erected in the main square and Picasso was invited to decorate a small chapel, which had fallen into disuse. Renewed by his contact with the Mediterranean, and by the challenges of yet another medium, he rediscovered, as Leymarie has it, 'the age-old secret of the potter's village, the unity of form and decoration, and then proceeded to remold form with his infallible touch.' By this time, Picasso had become very active in the peace movement, and his dove of peace was a familiar sight on posters and programs circulated by the movement. The birth of his two younger children was also the occasion for a new cycle of '*Maternités.*'

After his separation from Françoise in 1954, Picasso purchased another, more elegant, studio-home, the Villa La Californie, in Cannes. The previous year he had met Jacqueline Roque at Perpignan, and the two were soon sharing his Parisian studio in the rue des Grands-Augustins. In 1955 Picasso's first wife, Olga, from whom he had been separated since 1935, died at Cannes; his relationship with Jacqueline would endure for the rest of his life, despite the 47-year difference in their ages. She would be the subject of innumerable works during the nearly two decades that followed, including *Jacqueline in a Rocking Chair.* The two were married in 1958.

The year 1954 had brought the news of the death of Matisse, Picasso's old friend and rival, of whom he often said '*Au fond, il n'y a que Matisse*' ('All things considered, there's only Matisse'). Perhaps this loss was a factor in the cycle of variations on old masters that followed. On 13 December Picasso started work on a series of fifteen variations on Delacroix's painting *The Women of Algiers in their Apartment.* The series was completed by February 1955. This was not the first time Picasso had taken the theme or subject of a painting and used it as the basis for his variations in his own method and style. Other examples came from diverse sources: Le Nain, Renoir, Poussin, Lucas Cranach, Courbet and El Greco had all contributed. These variations would be followed by a series of 58 works on Velasquez's *Las Meniñas,* and *Déjeuner sur l'Herbe* after Monet and Manet.

Left: Poster for the second World Peace Congress, 1950. Picasso was active in the peace movement and the dove of peace became a familiar sight on programs and posters for the movement.

Below: Mother and Children (1953). The theme of motherhood, which had periodically occupied an important place in Picasso's work, reappeared during the childhood of Claude and Paloma. Private collection.

Above: Déjeuner sur l'Herbe (1863) by Edouard Manet. Picasso's painting from 1950-1963 was linked by variations on the old masters such as Delacroix, Velasquez and Manet. The theme of bathers was taken up by artists throughout the nineteenth and twentieth century. Musée Dorsay, Paris.

Left: Déjeuner sur l'Herbe by Claude Monet. The Impressionist Monet also produced his variation on a theme. Picasso would continue the subject through 27 paintings, 140 drawings, 3 linocuts and 10 cardboard maquettes for sculpture. Pushkin Museum of Art, Moscow.

Despite there being two versions of Delacroix's *Woman of Algiers* (one in the Louvre and another in Montpellier), Picasso stated that he had not seen either for several years, and claimed to have worked without the aid of reproductions, but simply allowing his 'visual memory' to guide him. In rapid succession Picasso painted the variations; some are in monochrome, others in vivid color. The same trend, beginning with representational studies and ending at near abstractions in the later works can be found again in the series based on *Las Meniñas,* painted three years later. These years also marked a return to familiar themes such as the studio, painter and model, and saw the unveiling of two monumental sculptures in the United States – at Chicago's civic centre and New York University. In addition, in the summer of 1953 Picasso became the sole star performer in the film *Le Mystère Picasso,* produced by Georges Clouzot.

The concentration on themes was relieved during this period of painting with studies of landscape and the doves which nested on the balcony of his studio. These paintings of bright Mediterranean light contrast with the dark interiors of the Spanish court paintings.

Picasso's friend and biographer David Douglas Duncan admits candidly in his centennial tribute *Viva Picasso,* published in 1981, that the artist was 'the most negligent of fathers, whose paternal interest generally surfaced during school holidays and summer vacations, when his children's visits to the studio were the least disruptive to his work.' Claude and Paloma lived in Paris with their mother for most of the year, but they made long visits to the

Riviera during the summer holidays and figured in many paintings and drawings. In 1958 Picasso purchased the stately home that Duncan describes as 'the remote and austere Château de Vauvenargues,' along with 'most of the northern slopes of Ste Victoire, ''Cézanne's mountain,'' near Aix-en-Provence . . . the harsh landscape surrounding the château probably reminded him of Spain, which he would never see again.' Picasso and Jacqueline lived here for only two years; then, finding it too remote, they removed briefly to La Californie before purchasing another home, Notre-Dame-de-Vie, in Mougins. This sprawling villa near Cannes, shaded by olive trees, would be Picasso's home for most of his remaining years. But as Duncan points out, 'Pablo never sold any of his studio-homes; instead he gave them to members of his family, or kept them . . . until the end.'

The end came at Notre-Dame-de-Vie, on 8 April 1973, when Picasso was almost 92 years old. 'He had worked,' recalls Duncan, 'until nearly daylight the morning he died.' The artist who had etched *The Frugal Repast* in 1904 left an estate valued at $166 million. He was buried at the foot of the grand staircase outside the Château de Vauvenargues, in a plot marked only by his bronze figure of an earth mother *Woman with Vase,* which he had cast in 1933. Two years before his death, his friend Leymarie had written what could have been his epitaph, had he needed one:

He has outlived his revolution and goes on marking the century with his inexhaustible powers of self-renewal and the sovereignty of his genius, in the solitary and authoritative manner of Michelangelo.

Above: This picture was taken in 1955, the year Picasso's first wife, Olga, died, and the year Picasso would move to Villa Californie, near Cannes.

Right: In May 1962 Picasso was awarded the Lenin peace prize for the second time. The theme of the dove continued in his work, both as the symbol of peace and in paintings of doves perching on the balcony of his studio.

In the Dressing-Room
1900, pastel on paper, 18⅞×20⅞in (48×53cm)
Picasso Museum, Barcelona

The Embrace in the Street   (page 27)
1900, pastel on paper, 22¼×13¾in (59×35cm)
Picasso Museum, Barcelona

Self-portrait   (page 24)
1901, oil on canvas, 31×23⅝in (79×60cm)
Picasso Museum, Paris

Sabartés as a 'Decadent Poet'   (page 25)
1900, charcoal and watercolor on paper, 18⅞×12½in (48×32cm)
Picasso Museum, Barcelona

Salón del Prado
1897, oil on wood, 25⅜×60⅛in (65×154cm)
Picasso Museum, Barcelona

Child with a Dove
1901, oil on canvas, 28⅜×21¼in (73×54cm)
Anonymous loan to the National Gallery, London

The Tragedy
1903, oil on wood, 41½×27⅛in (105.4×69cm)
National Gallery of Art, Washington
Chester Dale Collection

Circus Artist and Child
1905, watercolor drawing on paper, 6⅞×4⅛in (16.8×10.5cm)
Tate Gallery, London

The Death of Casagemas
1901, oil on wood, 10⅝×13⅞in (27×35cm)
Picasso Museum, Paris

The Soler Family (Le Déjeuner sur l'Herbe)
1903, oil on canvas, 59×78¾in (150×200cm)
Liège Musée des Beaux Arts, Paris

The Two Brothers
Summer 1906, gouache on cardboard, 31½×23¼in (80×59cm)
Picasso Museum, Paris

Girl in a Chemise
*c*1905, oil on canvas, 28⅝×23⅝in (72.7×60cm)
Tate Gallery, London

**Spanish Woman from the Island of Majorca
(Sketch for painting 'Les Bateleurs')**
1905, gouache on cardboard, 29½×20in (75×51cm)
Pushkin Fine Arts Museum, Moscow

Manola with Pointillist Technique
1917, oil on canvas, 46½×35in (118×89cm)
Picasso Museum, Barcelona

Portrait of Olga in an Armchair
Fall 1917, oil on canvas, 51¼×35in (130×88.8cm)
Picasso Museum, Paris

Woman in a Hat
1921, charcoal and pastel on canvas, 51¼×38¼in (130×97cm)
Picasso Museum, Paris

Three Women at the Fountain
Summer 1921, sanguine on canvas, 78¾×63⅜in (200×161cm)
Picasso Museum, Paris

The Bathers
Summer 1918, oil on canvas, 10⅝×8¾in (27×22cm)
Picasso Museum, Paris

Two Women Running on the Beach (The Race)
Summer 1922, gouache on plywood, 12⅞×16¼in (32.5×41.1cm)
Picasso Museum, Paris

Seated Woman in a Chemise
1923, oil on canvas, 36¼×28¾in (92.1×73cm)
Tate Gallery, London

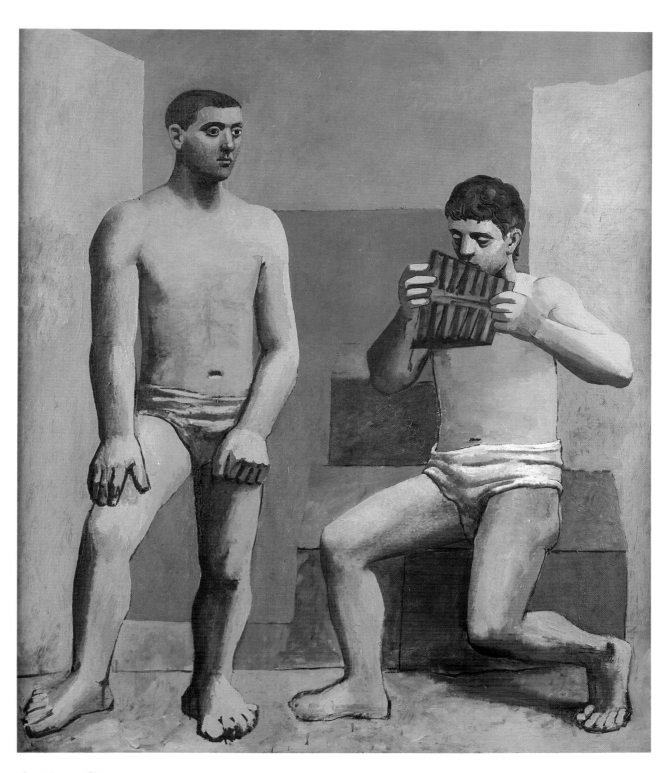

The Pipes of Pan
Summer 1923, oil on canvas, 80¾×68½in (205×174cm)
Picasso Museum, Paris

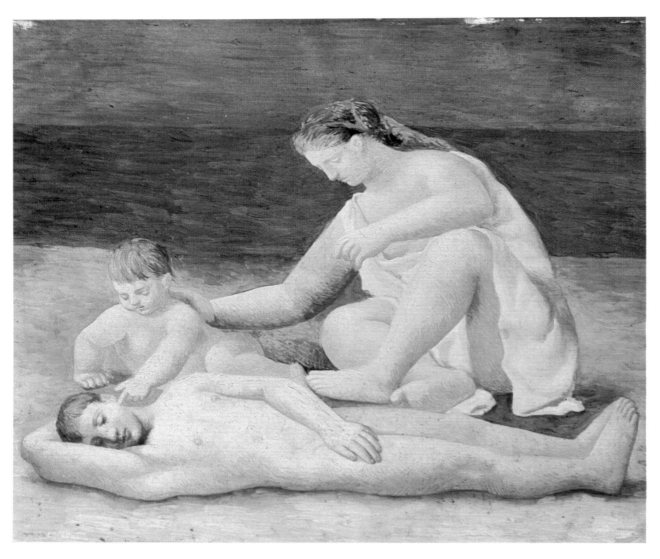

Family on the Seashore
Summer 1922, oil on wood panel, 6⅞×8in (17.6×20.2cm)
Picasso Museum, Paris

Paul as Harlequin   (page 48)
1924, oil on canvas, 52×38¾in (132×98.4cm)
Picasso Museum, Paris

Paul as Pierrot   (page 49)
28 February 1925, oil on canvas, 51¼×38¼in (130×97cm)
Picasso Museum, Paris

Harlequin with a Mirror
1923, oil on canvas, 39½×32in (100.3×81.3cm)
Thyssen-Bornemisza Collection, Lugano

Guitar, Gas Jet and Bottle
1912-13, oil, sand on canvas, 27¾×21⅞in (70.4×55.3cm)
Scottish National Gallery of Modern Art

Man with a Clarinet
1911-12, oil on canvas, 41¼×27⅛in (105×69cm)
Thyssen-Bornemisza Collection, Lugano

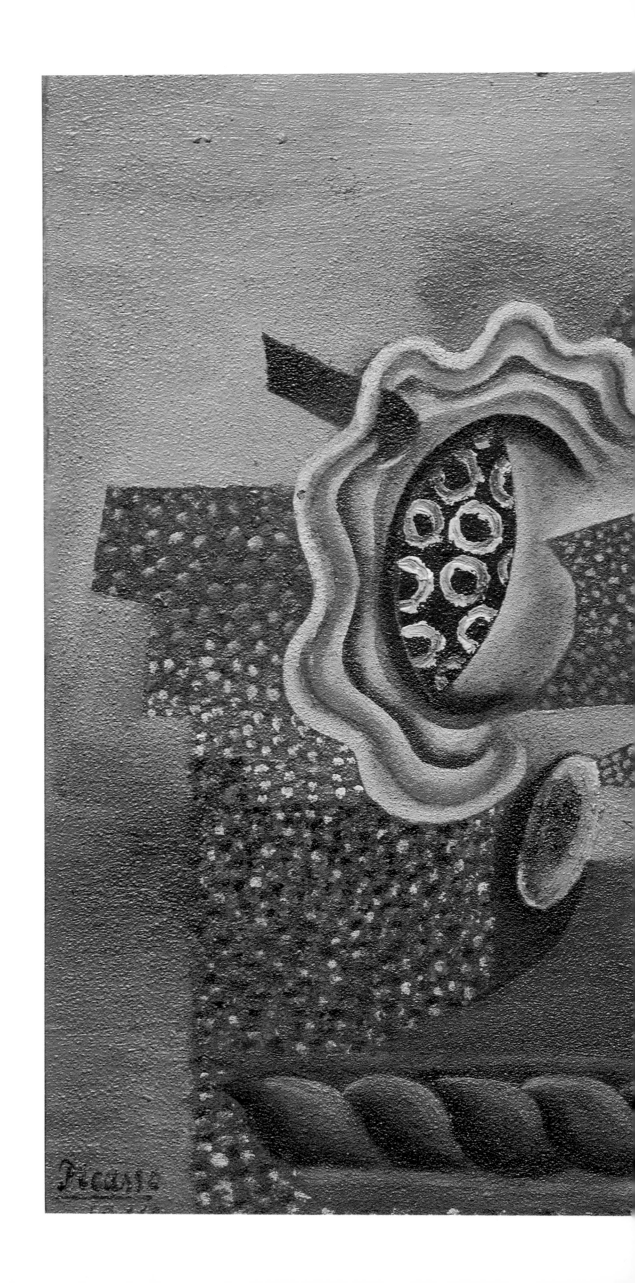

Still-life with Grapes and Pear
1914, oil on board
Private collection

The Swimmer
November 1929, oil on canvas, 51¼×63⅞in (130×162cm)
Picasso Museum, Paris

The Painter and his Model   (pages 54-55)
1926, oil on canvas, 67¾×100⅞in (172×256cm)
Picasso Museum, Paris

Sketch for Guernica
1937, pencil on paper
The Prado, Madrid

Guernica (overleaf)
1937, oil on canvas, 138×308in (350.0×782.3cm)
The Prado, Madrid

Sketch for Guernica
1937, crayon and pencil on paper
The Prado, Madrid

The Kiss
Summer 1925, oil on canvas, 51⅜×38½ (130.5×97.7cm)
Picasso Museum, Paris

Reclining Nude
4 April 1932, oil on canvas, 51¼×63¾in (130×161.7cm)
Picasso Museum, Paris

Woman in a Red Armchair
27 January 1932, oil on canvas, 51¼×38¼in (130.2×97cm)
Picasso Museum, Paris

Figures on the Seashore   (pages 62-63)
12 January 1931, oil on canvas, 51¼×76⅞in (130×195cm)
Picasso Museum, Paris

Large Still-life with a Pedestal Table
11 March 1931, oil on canvas, 76⅞×51⅜in (195×130.5cm)
Picasso Museum, Paris

Nude Woman in a Red Armchair
1932, oil on canvas, 58⅛×38¼in (129.9×97.2cm)
Tate Gallery, London

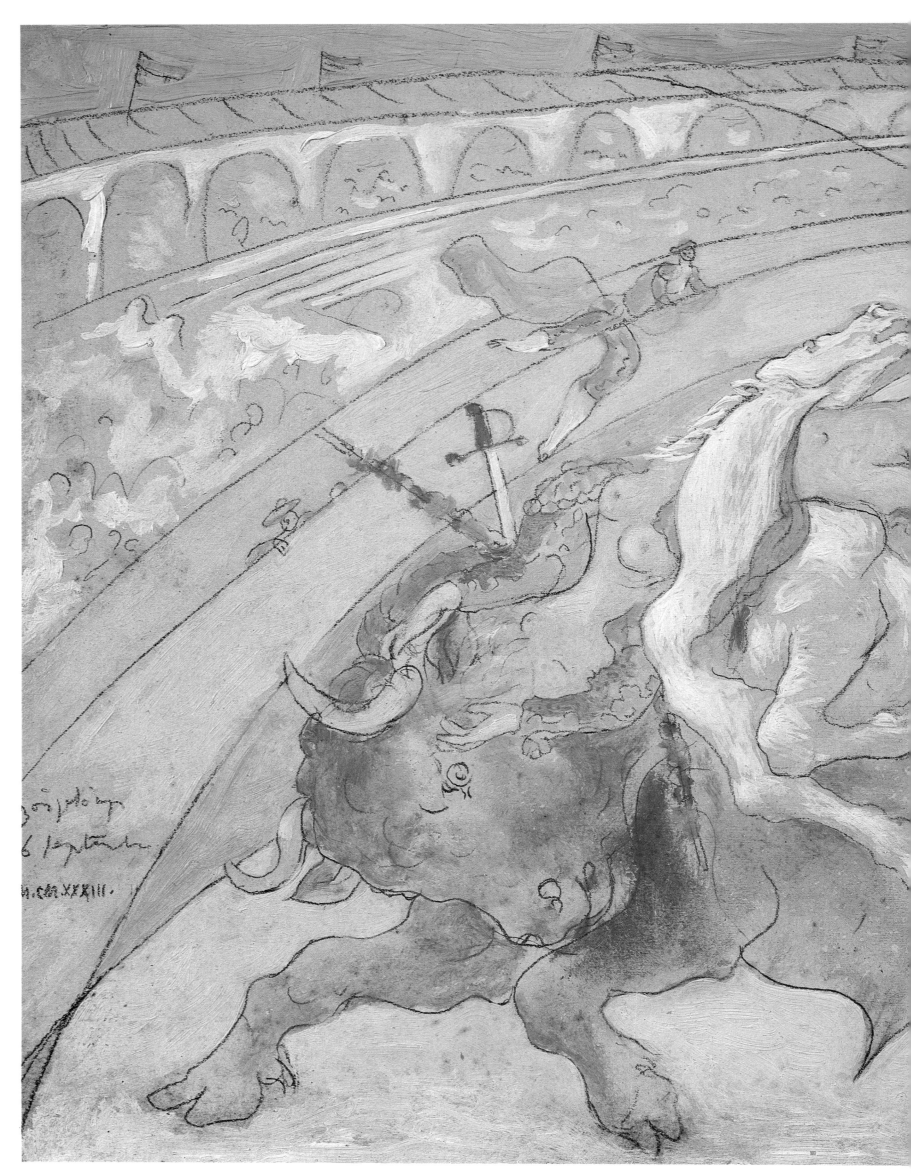

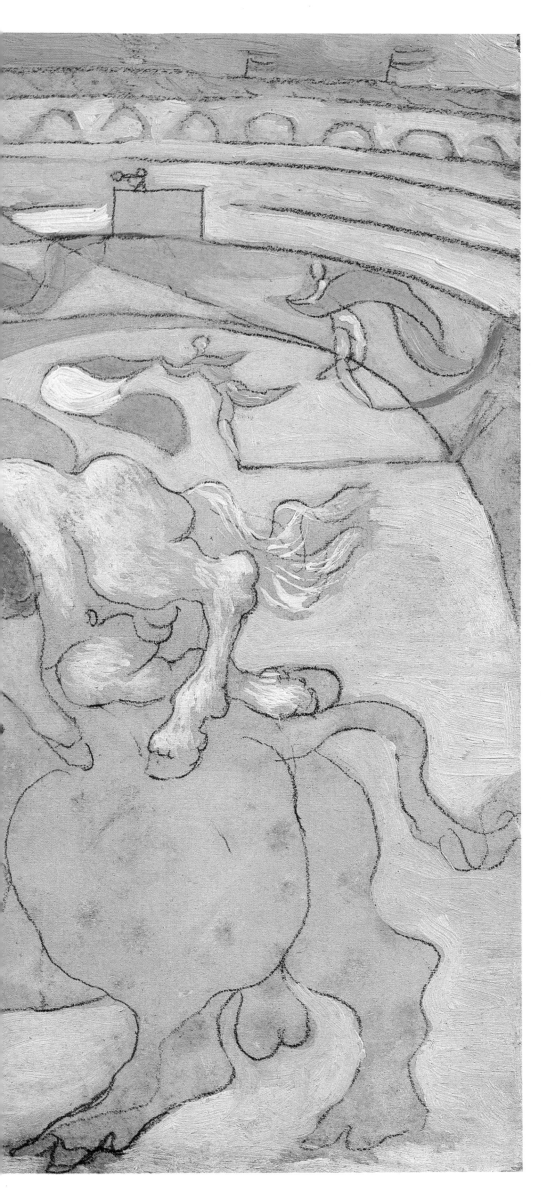

Bullfight: Death of the Woman Toreador
6 September 1933, oil and crayon on wood panel
8½×10⅝in (21.7×27cm)
Picasso Museum, Paris

The Crucifixion
7 February 1930, oil on plywood
20¼×26¼in (51.5×66.5cm)
Picasso Museum, Paris

Nude on the Terrace
16 July 1933, watercolor and india ink on paper
15¾×20in (40×50.8cm)
Private collection

Portrait of Dora Maar
1936, oil on canvas, 25½×21¼in (65×54cm)
Private collection, Paris

Dora Maar Seated
1938, watercolor, gouache and oil on paper, 27⅛×17½in (68.9×44.5cm)
Tate Gallery, London

Seated Woman in front of a Window
11 March 1937, oil and pastel on canvas, 51¼×38¼in (130×97.3cm)
Picasso Museum, Paris

Portrait of Dora Maar
1937, oil on canvas, 36¼×25⅝in (92×65cm)
Picasso Museum, Paris

Maya with her Doll
16 January 1938, oil on canvas, 28⅞×23⅝in (73.5×60cm)
Picasso Museum, Paris

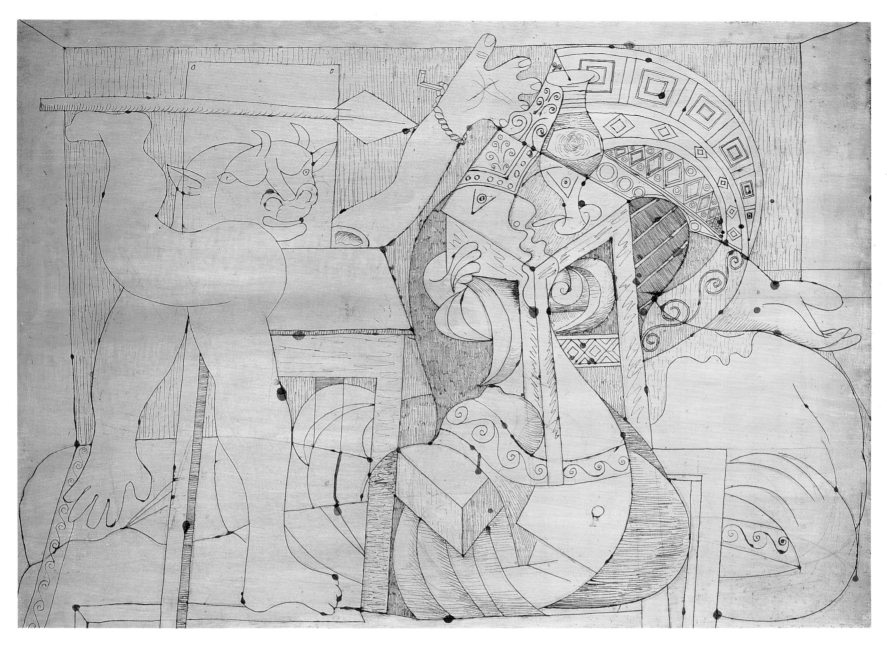

Minotaur with a Javelin
25 January 1934, india ink on plywood, 38¼×51¼in (97×130cm)
Picasso Museum, Paris

Café at Royan
1940, oil on canvas
38¼×15¼in (97.2×38.7cm)
Picasso Museum, Paris

Goat's Skull, Bottle and Candle
1952, oil on canvas, 35⅛×45¾in (89.2×116.2cm)
Tate Gallery, London

Head of a Faun
1947, gouache
Private collection

First Steps
1943, oil on canvas, 51¼×38¼in (130.2×97.2cm)
Yale University Art Gallery
Gift of Stephen C Clark, BA. 1903

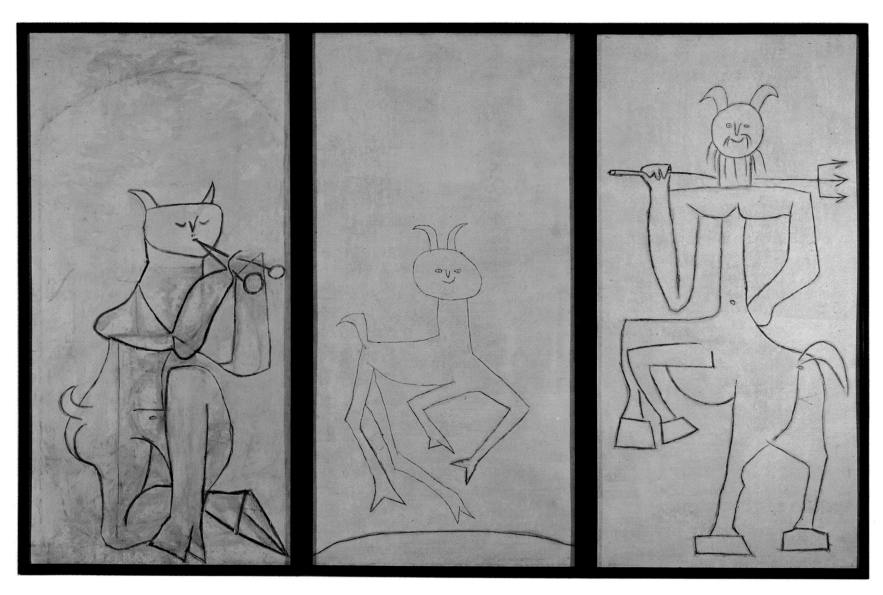

Triptych: Satyr, Faun and Centaur
1946, oil drawing on fibrocement, each 98¾×47¼in (250.8×120cm)
Picasso Museum, Antibes

Blue Owl
1947, oil on canvas, 48⅜×40¼in (123×102cm)
Private collection

Two Children (Claude Drawing with Paloma)
1952, oil on canvas, 36¼×28¾in (92.1×73cm)
Private collection

Jacqueline in a Rocking Chair
1954, oil on canvas, 57⅛×44⅞in (146×114cm)
Private collection

Spring
1956, oil on canvas, 51×76½in (129.5×194.3cm)
Private collection, Paris

Women of Algiers [after Delacroix]
14 February 1955, oil on canvas, 44⅞×57½in (113.8×146.1cm)
Collection of Mr and Mrs Victor W Ganz, New York

Women of Algiers [after Delacroix]
1 January 1955, oil on canvas, 18×21½in (45.7×54.6cm)
Private collection

Las Meninas (The Maids of Honor, after Velásquez)
17 August 1957, oil on canvas, 76⅜×102⅜in (194.1×260.1cm)
Picasso Museum, Barcelona

The Infanta Margarita
1957, oil on canvas, 39⅜×32in (100×81cm)
Picasso Museum, Barcelona

Las Meninas [The Doves, 1]
6 September 1957, oil on canvas, 31½×39⅜in (80×100cm)
Picasso Museum, Barcelona

Las Meninas [The Doves, 6]
12 September 1957, oil on canvas, 36⅞×44½in (145×113cm)
Picasso Museum, Barcelona

The Rape of the Sabine Women [after David]
4 November 1962, oil on canvas, 38¼×51¼in (97.2×130.2cm)
National Museum of Modern Art, Paris

Painter and Model
1970, colored crayon and chalk on cardboard, 8½×11⅛in (21.8×28.2cm)
Private collection

Le Déjeuner sur l'Herbe [after Manet]   (pages 100-101)
3 March - 20 August 1960, oil on canvas, 51¼×76⅞in (130×195cm)
Picasso Museum, Paris

The Kiss
26 October 1969, oil on canvas
38¼×51¼in (97×130cm)
Picasso Museum, Paris

The Matador
4 October 1970, oil on canvas, 57¼×44⅞in (145.5×114cm)
Picasso Museum, Paris

The Family
30 September 1970, oil on canvas, 63⅞×51¼in (162×130cm)
Picasso Museum, Paris

Violin
Late December 1913 - early 1914, cardboard box, pasted papers, gouache,
charcoal and chalk on paper 20¼×12in (51.5×30.4cm)
Picasso Museum, Paris

Mandolin and Clarinet
Fall 1913, construction: fir components with paint and crayon strokes
22⅞×14¼×9⅛in (58×36×23cm)
Picasso Museum, Paris

Glass, Pipe, Ace of Clubs and Die
Summer, 1914, painted wooden and metal components on wooden base
painted in oils 13⅜[diameter]×3¼in (34[diameter]×8.5cm)
Picasso Museum, Paris

Man with a Pipe
Spring 1914, oil on printed textile pasted on
canvas, 54¼×26¼in (138×66.5cm)
Picasso Museum, Paris

Bust of a Woman
1931, bronze (unique cast), 30¾×17½×21¼in (78×44.5×54cm)
Picasso Museum, Paris

Man with Sheep
1943, bronze, 87⅝×30¾×30¾in (222.5×78×78cm)
Picasso Museum, Paris

Head of a Woman
1929-30, painted iron, sheet-iron, springs and colanders
39⅜×14⅝×23¼in (100×37×59cm)

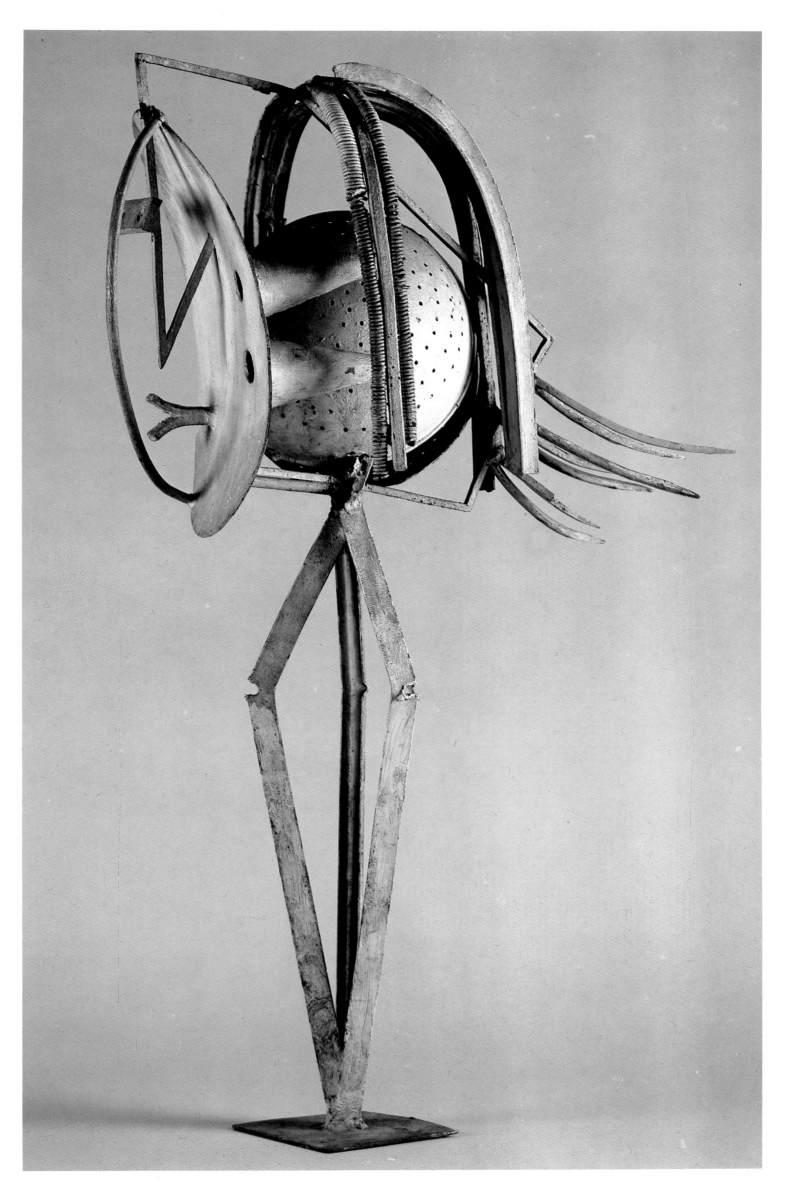

The publisher would like to thank
Adrian Hodgkins the designer and the
staff at Musées Nationeaux, Paris, and
the Picasso Museum, Barcelona, for
their invaluable assistance with this
book.

All pictures were provided by the
credited museum or gallery, except
those supplied by the following
agencies:

Art Resource: pages 10 (both), 11
(left), 14 (below right), 20 (below), 34,
47, 51, 89, 90, 92-93, 109

Art Resource/Giraudon: pages 14 (top
left), 19 (top & below), 20 (top), 24,
74, 86, 94, 98

Art Resource/Scala: pages 22, 88, 91

Art Resource/SPADEM Phototheque:
page 46

BBC Hulton Picture Library: page 23
(below left)

Bettmann Archive: pages 11 (right),
15, 16 (top), 18, 23 (top), 85, 87

Bulloz: page 12 (top)

E T Archive: pages 52-53, 95

The Keystone Collection: pages 17
(right), 23 (below right)

Peter Newark's Historical Pictures;
page 17 (top left)

Novosti Press Agency: pages 21
(below), 37